Broken & Redeemed

A STUDY ON THE GOD WHO REDEEMS OUR STORIES

Contents

Welcome

WE ARE GLAD you have decided to join us in this Bible study! First of all, please know that you have been prayed for! It is not a coincidence you are participating in this study.

Our prayer for you is simple: that you will grow closer to our Lord as you dig into His Word each and every day! As you develop the discipline of being in God's Word on a daily basis, our prayer is that you will fall in love with Him even more as you spend time reading from the Bible.

Each day before you read the assigned scripture(s), pray and ask God to help you understand it. Invite Him to speak to you through His Word. Then listen. It's His job to speak to you, and it's your job to listen and obey.

Take time to read the verses over and over again. We are told in Proverbs to search and you will find: "Search for it like silver, and hunt for it like hidden treasure. Then you will understand" (Prov. 2:4–5 NCV).

We are thrilled to provide these different resources for you as you participate in our online Bible study:

- *Broken & Redeemed* Study Journal

- Reading Plan

- Weekly Blog Posts (Mondays, Wednesdays, and Fridays)

- Weekly Memory Verses

- Weekly Monday Videos

- Weekly Challenges

- Online Community: Facebook, Twitter, Instagram, LoveGodGreatly.com

- Hashtags: #LoveGodGreatly

All of us here at Love God Greatly can't wait for you to get started, and we hope to see you at the finish line. Endure, persevere, press on—and don't give up! Finish well what you are beginning today. We will be here every step of the way, cheering you on! We are in this together. Fight to rise early, to push back the stress of the day, to sit alone and spend time in God's Word! Let's see what God has in store for you in this study! Journey with us as we learn to love God greatly with our lives!

Our Community

LOVE GOD GREATLY (LGG) is a beautiful community of women who use a variety of technology platforms to keep each other accountable in God's Word.

We start with a simple Bible reading plan, but it doesn't stop there.

Some women gather in homes and churches locally, while others connect online with women across the globe. Whatever the method, we lovingly lock arms and unite for this purpose: to love God greatly with our lives.

In today's fast-paced technology-driven world, it would be easy to study God's Word in an isolated environment that lacks encouragement or support, but that isn't the intention here at Love God Greatly. God created us to live in community with Him and with those around us.

We need each other, and we live life better together.

Because of this, would you consider reaching out and doing this study with someone?

All of us have women in our lives who need friendship, accountability, and have the desire to dive into God's Word on a deeper level. Rest assured we'll be studying right alongside you—learning with you, cheering for you, enjoying sweet fellowship, and smiling from ear to ear as we watch God unite women together—intentionally connecting hearts and minds for His glory.

It's pretty unreal, this opportunity we have to grow not only closer to God through this study but also to each other. So here's the challenge: call your mom, your sister, your grandma, the girl across the street, or the college friend across the country. Gather a group of girls from your church or workplace, or meet in a coffee shop with friends you have always wished you knew better. Utilize the beauty of connecting online for inspiration and accountability, and take opportunities to meet in person when you can.

Arm-in-arm and hand-in-hand, let's do this thing...together.

How to SOAP

We really want you to know that.

We're proud of you for making the commitment to be in God's Word, to be reading it each day and applying it to your life, the beautiful life our Lord has given you.

In this study we offer you a study journal to accompany the verses we are reading. This journal is designed to help you interact with God's Word and learn to dig deeper, encouraging you to slow down and reflect on what God is saying to you that day.

At Love God Greatly, we use the SOAP Bible study method. Before beginning, let's take a moment to define this method and share why we recommend using it during your quiet time.

Why SOAP It?

It's one thing to simply read Scripture. But when you interact with it, intentionally slowing down to really reflect on it, suddenly words start popping off the page. The SOAP method allows you to dig deeper into Scripture and see more than you would if you simply read the verses and then went on your merry way. Please take the time to SOAP through our Bible studies and see for yourself how much more you get from your daily reading. You'll be amazed.

What Does SOAP Mean?

S stands for **Scripture**. Physically write out the verses. You'll be amazed at what God will reveal to you just by taking the time to slow down and write out what you are reading!

O stands for **observation**. What do you see in the verses that you're reading? Who is the intended audience? Is there a repetition of words? What words stand out to you?

A stands for **application**. This is when God's Word becomes personal. What is God saying to you today? How can you apply what you just read to your own personal life? What changes do you need to make? Is there action you need to take?

P stands for **prayer**. Pray God's Word back to Him. Spend time thanking Him. If He has revealed something to you during this time in His Word, pray about it. If He has revealed some sin that is in your life, confess. And remember, He loves you dearly.

Follow This Example

Scripture: Read and write out Colossians 1:5–8.

> "The faith and love that spring from the hope stored up for you in heaven and about which you have already heard in the true message of the gospel that has come to you. In the same way, the gospel is bearing fruit and growing throughout the whole world— just as it has been doing among you since the day you heard it and truly understood God's grace. You learned it from Epaphras, our dear fellow servant, who is a faithful minister of Christ on our behalf, and who also told us of your love in the Spirit" (NIV).

Observation: Write what stands out to you.

> When you combine faith and love, you get hope. We must remember that our hope is in heaven; it is yet to come. The gospel is the Word of truth. The gospel is continually bearing fruit and growing from the first day to the last. It just takes one person to change a whole community...Epaphras.

Application: Apply this scripture to your own life.

> God used one man, Epaphras, to change a whole town. I was reminded that we are simply called to tell others about Christ; it's God's job to spread the gospel, to grow it, and have it bear fruit. I felt today's verses were almost directly spoken to Love God Greatly women: "The gospel is bearing fruit and growing throughout the whole world—just as it has been doing among you since the day you heard it and truly understood God's grace."

It's so fun when God's Word comes alive and encourages us in our current situation! My passionate desire is that all the women involved in our LGG Bible study will understand God's grace and have a thirst for His Word. I was moved by this quote from my Bible commentary today: "God's Word is not just for our information, it is for our transformation."

Prayer: Pray over this.

> Dear Lord, please help me to be an "Epaphras," to tell others about You and then leave the results in Your loving hands. Please help me to understand and apply personally what I have read today to my life, thereby becoming more and more like You each and every day. Help me to live a life that bears the fruit of faith and love, anchoring my hope in heaven, not here on earth. Help me to remember that the best is yet to come!

SOAP It Up

Remember, the most important ingredients in the SOAP method are your interaction with God's Word and your application of His Word to your life:

> Blessed is the one who does not walk in step with the wicked or stand in the way that sinners take or sit in the company of mockers, but whose delight is in the law of the LORD, and who meditates on his law day and night. That person is like a tree planted by streams of water, which yields its fruit in season and whose leaf does not wither—whatever they do prospers. (Ps. 1:1–3, NIV)

Reading Plan

WEEK 1 - Naomi - Loss/loneliness

Monday	Read: Ruth 1	SOAP: Ruth 1:20-21
Tuesday	Read: Psalm 119:25-32	SOAP: Psalm 119:28
Wednesday	Read: Psalm 34	SOAP: Psalm 34:17-18
Thursday	Read: Revelation 21:1-6	SOAP: Revelation 21:4
Friday	Read: Psalm 42	SOAP: Psalm 42:11
Response Day		

WEEK 2 - Moses - fear and weakness

Monday	Read: Exodus 3:1-15	SOAP: Exodus 3:11-14
Tuesday	Read: Exodus 4:1-17	SOAP: Exodus 4:10-13
Wednesday	Read: Deuteronomy 31:1-8	SOAP: Deuteronomy 31:7-8
Thursday	Read: Isaiah 40:28-31	SOAP: Isaiah 40:28-31
Friday	Read: Isaiah 41:9-10	SOAP: Isaiah 41:10
Response Day		

WEEK 3 - Sarah - infertility

Monday	Read: Genesis 17:15-19; Genesis 18:9-15	SOAP: Genesis 18:12-14a
Tuesday	Read: Psalm 55	SOAP: Psalm 55:22
Wednesday	Read: Psalm 73	SOAP: Psalm 73:25-26
Thursday	Read: Psalm 119:68; Psalm 34:8-11	SOAP: Psalm 119:68
Friday	Read: 2 Corinthians 4:7-11	SOAP: 2 Corinthians 4:7-9
Response Day		

WEEK 4 - Paul - misplaced zeal and pride

Monday	Read: Galatians 1:11-14	SOAP: Galatians 1:14
Tuesday	Read: Galatians 6:11-16	SOAP: Galatians 6:14-15
Wednesday	Read: 1 Corinthians 1:26-31	SOAP: 1 Corinthians 1:30-31
Thursday	Read: James 4:6-10	SOAP: James 4:6
Friday	Read: Titus 2:11-14	SOAP: Titus 2:14
Response Day		

WEEK 5 - The Adulterous Woman

Monday	Read: John 8:1-11	SOAP: John 8:10-11
Tuesday	Read: Romans 8:1-11	SOAP: Romans 8:1-2
Wednesday	Read: Psalm 103	SOAP: Psalm 103:11-13
Thursday	Read: Psalm 27	SOAP: Psalm 27:7-8
Friday	Read: James 4:1-4	SOAP: James 4:4
Response Day		

WEEK 6 - Jesus - Broken and Raised For Us

Monday	Read: Isaiah 53	SOAP: Isaiah 53:4-5
Tuesday	Read: Matthew 26:17-29	SOAP: Matthew 26:26-27
Wednesday	Read: John 19:16-30	SOAP: John 19:28-30
Thursday	Read: Hebrews 12:1-3	SOAP: Hebrews 12:3
Friday	Read: 1 Corinthians 15:1-4	SOAP: 1 Corinthians 15:3-4
Response Day		

Goals

WE BELIEVE it's important to write out goals for this study. Take some time now and write three goals you would like to focus on as you begin to rise each day and dig into God's Word. Make sure and refer back to these goals throughout the next six weeks to help you stay focused. You can do it!

My goals are:

1.

2.

3.

Signature: _____

Date: _____

Introduction

Broken

IT MEANS TO BE damaged or no longer in proper working order. You see it in illnesses that ravage a once energetic and lively body. You see it in families where marriages are fractured. You see it in relationships that suffer from intentional, or even unintentional hurt. Brokenness is identified in tears and death, in suffering and heartache, in damage and decay. It often results in anger or greed, in selfishness or loneliness, or even in despair.

Brokenness is *all around* us. No matter how hard we try we can never escape it, because we all carry brokenness *within* us.

And it's all because of sin.

In C.S. Lewis' book *The Lion, The Witch, and the Wardrobe*, an evil witch turns those with whom she is displeased into stone statues. Her victims are alive but can do nothing. *They need to be rescued.* This is what sin has done to our hearts. Hearts that once beat for the love of God have been petrified so they cannot truly love God. Sin has created a wedge between man and God and between man and man. The difference is that a witch did not do this to us. *We did it to ourselves.*

Like a prison guard, sin has wrapped us in chains and has stamped us with a seal of guilt that we cannot break or remove. Sin is all darkness, all heinousness, all evil. Everything on earth has been taken captive by this curse and it destroys everything it touches.

Throughout Scripture we read stories of broken people. From Adam to the apostle Paul, all were hopeless on their own. But the beauty of God's Word is that it is not just a story of tragedy. **Woven throughout the Bible is also the greatest story of redemption.**

Redeemed

BUT GOD!

But God, being rich in mercy,
because of the great love with which he loved us,
even when we were dead in our trespasses,
made us alive together with Christ —
by grace you have been saved.

- Ephesians 2:4-5

In God there is always good news. He has not left His creation in sin. He did not ignore the brokenness of His people.

In the weeks to come we will see the goodness of God in that He did not forget Sarah throughout her years of infertility. We will see Him care for Naomi as she deals with loss and loneliness. Behold our great God who gave Moses courage, Paul true zeal, and the adulterous woman forgiveness and the chance of a new life.

While we see the mercy and kindness of God in these stories, they are only temporary helps. The issue of our brokenness goes beyond our physical and emotional well being. All of the people we will study - *and us included* - have hearts and souls that need rescuing; otherwise our brokenness will never end. In God's work of restoration we experience love, joy, satisfaction, and freedom through Jesus Christ. **We will see that the answer to all of our brokenness, no matter what it is, is Christ himself.**

Throughout the entire Old Testament we find God's promise that a Savior is coming - a Redeemer whose sacrifice would break the chain of sin and whose blood would melt the heart of stone. While brokenness - in the sense that we see it here on earth - will no longer be a part of our reality in heaven, we will see the evidence of Christ's brokenness for us on a daily basis. His hands, His feet, and His side will forever bear the scars of that horrendous death He went through for us. The proof of our redemption will be forever before us, and we will rejoice!

So grab your favorite beverage, crack open your Bible, and **together let's rejoice with the broken and redeemed of God.**

Week 1

Week 1 Challenge (Note: You can find this listed in our Monday blog post):

Prayer focus for this week: Spend time praying for your family members.

	Praying	Praise
Monday		
Tuesday		
Wednesday		
Thursday		
Friday		

The Lord is near to the brokenhearted
and saves the crushed in spirit.

PSALM 34:18

Scripture for Week 1

NAOMI - LOSS/LONELINESS

MONDAY

RUTH 1

[1] In the days when the judges ruled there was a famine in the land, and a man of Bethlehem in Judah went to sojourn in the country of Moab, he and his wife and his two sons. [2] The name of the man was Elimelech and the name of his wife Naomi, and the names of his two sons were Mahlon and Chilion. They were Ephrathites from Bethlehem in Judah. They went into the country of Moab and remained there. [3] But Elimelech, the husband of Naomi, died, and she was left with her two sons. [4] These took Moabite wives; the name of the one was Orpah and the name of the other Ruth. They lived there about ten years, [5] and both Mahlon and Chilion died, so that the woman was left without her two sons and her husband.

[6] Then she arose with her daughters-in-law to return from the country of Moab, for she had heard in the fields of Moab that the Lord had visited his people and given them food. [7] So she set out from the place where she was with her two daughters-in-law, and they went on the way to return to the land of Judah. [8] But Naomi said to her two daughters-in-law, "Go, return each of you to her mother's house. May the Lord deal kindly with you, as you have dealt with the dead and with me. [9] The Lord grant that you may find rest, each of you in the house of her husband!" Then she kissed them, and they lifted up their voices and wept. [10] And they said to her, "No, we will return with you to your people." [11] But Naomi said, "Turn back, my daughters; why will you go with me? Have I yet sons in my womb that they may become your husbands? [12] Turn back, my daughters; go your way, for I am too old to have a husband. If I should say I have hope, even if I should have a husband this night and should bear sons, [13] would you therefore wait till they were grown? Would you therefore refrain from marrying? No, my daughters, for it is exceedingly bitter to

me for your sake that the hand of the Lord has gone out against me."¹⁴ Then they lifted up their voices and wept again. And Orpah kissed her mother-in-law, but Ruth clung to her.

¹⁵ And she said, "See, your sister-in-law has gone back to her people and to her gods; return after your sister-in-law." ¹⁶ But Ruth said, "Do not urge me to leave you or to return from following you. For where you go I will go, and where you lodge I will lodge. Your people shall be my people, and your God my God. ¹⁷ Where you die I will die, and there will I be buried. May the Lord do so to me and more also if anything but death parts me from you." ¹⁸ And when Naomi saw that she was determined to go with her, she said no more.

¹⁹ So the two of them went on until they came to Bethlehem. And when they came to Bethlehem, the whole town was stirred because of them. And the women said, "Is this Naomi?" ²⁰ She said to them, "Do not call me Naomi; call me Mara, for the Almighty has dealt very bitterly with me. ²¹ I went away full, and the Lord has brought me back empty. Why call me Naomi, when the Lord has testified against me and the Almighty has brought calamity upon me?"

²² So Naomi returned, and Ruth the Moabite her daughter-in-law with her, who returned from the country of Moab. And they came to Bethlehem at the beginning of barley harvest.

TUESDAY

PSALM 119:25-32

²⁵ My soul clings to the dust;

   give me life according to your word!

²⁶ When I told of my ways, you answered me;

   teach me your statutes!

²⁷ Make me understand the way of your precepts,

   and I will meditate on your wondrous works.

²⁸ My soul melts away for sorrow;

   strengthen me according to your word!

²⁹ Put false ways far from me

and graciously teach me your law!

³⁰ I have chosen the way of faithfulness;

I set your rules before me.

³¹ I cling to your testimonies, O Lord;

let me not be put to shame!

³² I will run in the way of your commandments

when you enlarge my heart!

WEDNESDAY

PSALM 34

¹ I will bless the Lord at all times;

his praise shall continually be in my mouth.

² My soul makes its boast in the Lord;

let the humble hear and be glad.

³ Oh, magnify the Lord with me,

and let us exalt his name together!

⁴ I sought the Lord, and he answered me

and delivered me from all my fears.

⁵ Those who look to him are radiant,

and their faces shall never be ashamed.

⁶ This poor man cried, and the Lord heard him

and saved him out of all his troubles.

⁷ The angel of the Lord encamps

around those who fear him, and delivers them.

⁸ Oh, taste and see that the Lord is good!

Blessed is the man who takes refuge in him!

⁹ Oh, fear the Lord, you his saints,

for those who fear him have no lack!

¹⁰ The young lions suffer want and hunger;

but those who seek the Lord lack no good thing.

[11] Come, O children, listen to me;

I will teach you the fear of the Lord.

[12] What man is there who desires life

and loves many days, that he may see good?

[13] Keep your tongue from evil

and your lips from speaking deceit.

[14] Turn away from evil and do good;

seek peace and pursue it.

[15] The eyes of the Lord are toward the righteous

and his ears toward their cry.

[16] The face of the Lord is against those who do evil,

to cut off the memory of them from the earth.

[17] When the righteous cry for help, the Lord hears

and delivers them out of all their troubles.

[18] The Lord is near to the brokenhearted

and saves the crushed in spirit.

[19] Many are the afflictions of the righteous,

but the Lord delivers him out of them all.

[20] He keeps all his bones;

not one of them is broken.

[21] Affliction will slay the wicked,

and those who hate the righteous will be condemned.

[22] The Lord redeems the life of his servants;

none of those who take refuge in him will be condemned.

THURSDAY

REVELATION 21:1-6

[1] Then I saw a new heaven and a new earth, for the first heaven and the first earth had passed away, and the sea was no more. [2] And I saw the holy city, new Jerusalem, coming down out of heaven from God, prepared as a bride adorned for her husband. [3] And I heard a loud voice from the throne saying, "Behold, the dwelling place of God is with man. He will dwell with them, and they will be his people, and God himself will be with them as their God. [4] He will wipe away every tear from their eyes, and death shall be no more, neither shall there be mourning, nor crying, nor pain anymore, for the former things have passed away."

[5] And he who was seated on the throne said, "Behold, I am making all things new." Also he said, "Write this down, for these words are trustworthy and true." [6] And he said to me, "It is done! I am the Alpha and the Omega, the beginning and the end. To the thirsty I will give from the spring of the water of life without payment.

FRIDAY

PSALM 42

[1] As a deer pants for flowing streams,

so pants my soul for you, O God.

[2] My soul thirsts for God,

for the living God.

When shall I come and appear before God?

[3] My tears have been my food

day and night,

while they say to me all the day long,

"Where is your God?"

[4] These things I remember,

as I pour out my soul:

how I would go with the throng

and lead them in procession to the house of God

with glad shouts and songs of praise,

a multitude keeping festival.

⁵ Why are you cast down, O my soul,

and why are you in turmoil within me?

Hope in God; for I shall again praise him,

my salvation ⁶ and my God.

My soul is cast down within me;

therefore I remember you

from the land of Jordan and of Hermon,

from Mount Mizar.

⁷ Deep calls to deep

at the roar of your waterfalls;

all your breakers and your waves

have gone over me.

⁸ By day the Lord commands his steadfast love,

and at night his song is with me,

a prayer to the God of my life.

⁹ I say to God, my rock:

"Why have you forgotten me?

Why do I go mourning

because of the oppression of the enemy?"

¹⁰ As with a deadly wound in my bones,

my adversaries taunt me,

while they say to me all the day long,

"Where is your God?"

¹¹ Why are you cast down, O my soul,

and why are you in turmoil within me?

Hope in God; for I shall again praise him,

my salvation and my God.

Monday

READ: Ruth 1

SOAP: Ruth 1:20-21

Scripture - Write out the **Scripture** passage for the day.

Observations - Write down 1 or 2 **observations** from the passage.

Monday

Applications - Write down 1 or 2 **applications** from the passage.

Pray - Write out a **prayer** over what you learned from today's passage.

-Visit our website today for the corresponding blog post!-

Tuesday

READ: Psalm 119:25-32

SOAP: Psalm 119:28

Scripture - Write out the **Scripture** passage for the day.

Observations - Write down 1 or 2 **observations** from the passage.

Tuesday

Applications - Write down 1 or 2 **applications** from the passage.

Pray - Write out a **prayer** over what you learned from today's passage.

Wednesday

READ: Psalm 34

SOAP: Psalm 34:17-18

Scripture - Write out the **Scripture** passage for the day.

Observations - Write down 1 or 2 **observations** from the passage.

Wednesday

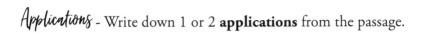

Applications - Write down 1 or 2 **applications** from the passage.

Pray - Write out a **prayer** over what you learned from today's passage.

-Visit our website today for the corresponding blog post!-

Thursday

READ: Revelation 21:1-6
SOAP: Revelation 21:4

Scripture - Write out the **Scripture** passage for the day.

Observations - Write down 1 or 2 **observations** from the passage.

Thursday

Applications - Write down 1 or 2 **applications** from the passage.

Pray - Write out a **prayer** over what you learned from today's passage.

Friday

READ: Psalm 42

SOAP: Psalm 42:11

Scripture - Write out the **Scripture** passage for the day.

Observations - Write down 1 or 2 **observations** from the passage.

Friday

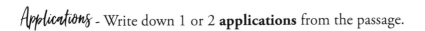

Applications - Write down 1 or 2 **applications** from the passage.

Pray - Write out a **prayer** over what you learned from today's passage.

-Visit our website today for the corresponding blog post!-

Reflection Questions

1. What does the name "Mara" mean and why does Naomi want to be called this?

2. According to Psalm 119, where can we find strength when we are worn out? In light of this, what should our priority be?

3. What does it mean that the Lord hears us? What does this mean for those who struggle with loneliness?

4. How does the future hope of Revelation 21:4 give us hope in our loneliness and loss today?

5. What truths about God's character can bring us comfort during times of loss?

My Response

Week 2

Week 2 Challenge (Note: You can find this listed in our Monday blog post):

Prayer focus for this week: Spend time praying for your country.

	Praying	Praise
Monday		
Tuesday		
Wednesday		
Thursday		
Friday		

"It is the Lord who goes before you.
He will be with you;
he will not leave you or forsake you.
Do not fear or be dismayed."

DEUTERONOMY 31:8

Scripture for Week 2

MOSES - FEAR AND WEAKNESS

MONDAY

EXODUS 3:1-15

¹ Now Moses was keeping the flock of his father-in-law, Jethro, the priest of Midian, and he led his flock to the west side of the wilderness and came to Horeb, the mountain of God. ² And the angel of the Lord appeared to him in a flame of fire out of the midst of a bush. He looked, and behold, the bush was burning, yet it was not consumed. ³ And Moses said, "I will turn aside to see this great sight, why the bush is not burned." ⁴ When the Lord saw that he turned aside to see, God called to him out of the bush, "Moses, Moses!" And he said, "Here I am." ⁵ Then he said, "Do not come near; take your sandals off your feet, for the place on which you are standing is holy ground." ⁶ And he said, "I am the God of your father, the God of Abraham, the God of Isaac, and the God of Jacob." And Moses hid his face, for he was afraid to look at God.

⁷ Then the Lord said, "I have surely seen the affliction of my people who are in Egypt and have heard their cry because of their taskmasters. I know their sufferings, ⁸ and I have come down to deliver them out of the hand of the Egyptians and to bring them up out of that land to a good and broad land, a land flowing with milk and honey, to the place of the Canaanites, the Hittites, the Amorites, the Perizzites, the Hivites, and the Jebusites. ⁹ And now, behold, the cry of the people of Israel has come to me, and I have also seen the oppression with which the Egyptians oppress them. ¹⁰ Come, I will send you to Pharaoh that you may bring my people, the children of Israel, out of Egypt." ¹¹ But Moses said to God, "Who am I that I should go to Pharaoh and bring the children of Israel out of Egypt?"¹² He said, "But I will be with you, and this shall be the sign for you, that I have sent you: when you have brought the people out of Egypt, you shall serve God on this mountain."

¹³ Then Moses said to God, "If I come to the people of Israel and say to them, 'The God of your fathers has sent me to you,' and they ask me, 'What is his name?' what shall I say to them?" ¹⁴ God said to Moses, "I am who I am." And he said, "Say this to the people of Israel: 'I am has sent me to you.'" ¹⁵ God also said to Moses, "Say this to the people of Israel: 'The Lord, the God of your fathers, the God of Abraham, the God of Isaac, and the God of Jacob, has sent me to you.' This is my name forever, and thus I am to be remembered throughout all generations.

TUESDAY

EXODUS 4:1-17

¹ Then Moses answered, "But behold, they will not believe me or listen to my voice, for they will say, 'The Lord did not appear to you.'"² The Lord said to him, "What is that in your hand?" He said, "A staff." ³ And he said, "Throw it on the ground." So he threw it on the ground, and it became a serpent, and Moses ran from it. ⁴ But the Lord said to Moses, "Put out your hand and catch it by the tail"—so he put out his hand and caught it, and it became a staff in his hand—⁵ "that they may believe that the Lord, the God of their fathers, the God of Abraham, the God of Isaac, and the God of Jacob, has appeared to you." ⁶ Again, the Lord said to him, "Put your hand inside your cloak." And he put his hand inside his cloak, and when he took it out, behold, his hand was leprous like snow. ⁷ Then God said, "Put your hand back inside your cloak." So he put his hand back inside his cloak, and when he took it out, behold, it was restored like the rest of his flesh. ⁸ "If they will not believe you," God said, "or listen to the first sign, they may believe the latter sign. ⁹ If they will not believe even these two signs or listen to your voice, you shall take some water from the Nile and pour it on the dry ground, and the water that you shall take from the Nile will become blood on the dry ground."

¹⁰ But Moses said to the Lord, "Oh, my Lord, I am not eloquent, either in the past or since you have spoken to your servant, but I am slow of speech and of tongue." ¹¹ Then the Lord said to him, "Who has made man's mouth? Who makes him mute, or deaf, or

seeing, or blind? Is it not I, the Lord? [12] Now therefore go, and I will be with your mouth and teach you what you shall speak." [13] But he said, "Oh, my Lord, please send someone else." [14] Then the anger of the Lord was kindled against Moses and he said, "Is there not Aaron, your brother, the Levite? I know that he can speak well. Behold, he is coming out to meet you, and when he sees you, he will be glad in his heart. [15] You shall speak to him and put the words in his mouth, and I will be with your mouth and with his mouth and will teach you both what to do. [16] He shall speak for you to the people, and he shall be your mouth, and you shall be as God to him. [17] And take in your hand this staff, with which you shall do the signs."

WEDNESDAY

DEUTERONOMY 31:1-8

[1] So Moses continued to speak these words to all Israel. [2] And he said to them, "I am 120 years old today. I am no longer able to go out and come in. The Lord has said to me, 'You shall not go over this Jordan.' [3] The Lord your God himself will go over before you. He will destroy these nations before you, so that you shall dispossess them, and Joshua will go over at your head, as the Lord has spoken. [4] And the Lord will do to them as he did to Sihon and Og, the kings of the Amorites, and to their land, when he destroyed them. [5] And the Lord will give them over to you, and you shall do to them according to the whole commandment that I have commanded you. [6] Be strong and courageous. Do not fear or be in dread of them, for it is the Lord your God who goes with you. He will not leave you or forsake you."

[7] Then Moses summoned Joshua and said to him in the sight of all Israel, "Be strong and courageous, for you shall go with this people into the land that the Lord has sworn to their fathers to give them, and you shall put them in possession of it. [8] It is the Lord who goes before you. He will be with you; he will not leave you or forsake you. Do not fear or be dismayed."

THURSDAY

ISAIAH 40:28-31

[28] Have you not known? Have you not heard?
The Lord is the everlasting God,
  the Creator of the ends of the earth.
He does not faint or grow weary;
  his understanding is unsearchable.
[29] He gives power to the faint,
  and to him who has no might he increases strength.
[30] Even youths shall faint and be weary,
  and young men shall fall exhausted;
[31] but they who wait for the Lord shall renew their strength;
  they shall mount up with wings like eagles;
they shall run and not be weary;
  they shall walk and not faint.

FRIDAY

ISAIAH 41:9-10

[9] you whom I took from the ends of the earth,
  and called from its farthest corners,
saying to you, "You are my servant,
  I have chosen you and not cast you off";
[10] fear not, for I am with you;
  be not dismayed, for I am your God;
I will strengthen you, I will help you,
  I will uphold you with my righteous right hand.

Monday

READ: Exodus 3:1-15

SOAP: Exodus 3:11-14

Scripture - Write out the **Scripture** passage for the day.

Observations - Write down 1 or 2 **observations** from the passage.

Monday

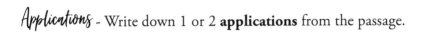

Applications - Write down 1 or 2 **applications** from the passage.

Pray - Write out a **prayer** over what you learned from today's passage.

-Visit our website today for the corresponding blog post!-

Tuesday

READ: Exodus 4:1-17

SOAP: Exodus 4:10-13

Scripture - Write out the **Scripture** passage for the day.

Observations - Write down 1 or 2 **observations** from the passage.

Tuesday

Applications - Write down 1 or 2 **applications** from the passage.

Pray - Write out a **prayer** over what you learned from today's passage.

READ: Deuteronomy 31:1-8
SOAP: Deuteronomy 31:7-8

Scripture - Write out the **Scripture** passage for the day.

Observations - Write down 1 or 2 **observations** from the passage.

Wednesday

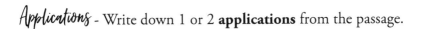

Applications - Write down 1 or 2 **applications** from the passage.

Pray - Write out a **prayer** over what you learned from today's passage.

Thursday

READ: Isaiah 40:28-31

SOAP: Isaiah 40:28-31

Scripture - Write out the **Scripture** passage for the day.

Observations - Write down 1 or 2 **observations** from the passage.

Thursday

Applications - Write down 1 or 2 **applications** from the passage.

Pray - Write out a **prayer** over what you learned from today's passage.

Friday

READ: Isaiah 41:9-10

SOAP: Isaiah 41:10

Scripture - Write out the **Scripture** passage for the day.

Observations - Write down 1 or 2 **observations** from the passage.

Friday

Applications - Write down 1 or 2 **applications** from the passage.

Pray - Write out a **prayer** over what you learned from today's passage.

-Visit our website today for the corresponding blog post!-

Reflection Questions

1. What weaknesses did Moses have that got in the way of him obeying God? What weaknesses do you have that keep you from obeying God?

2. In what truth about God is Moses supposed to find his boldness?

3. In Deuteronomy 31 Moses tells Joshua to be courageous because "The Lord goes before you." How does this knowledge produce courage?

4. According to Isaiah 40, how does our strength get renewed?

5. Fear keeps us from doing what God calls us to do. Think about the truths in Isaiah 41 and write down how these help you overcome fear:

   God is with you -

   He is your God -

   He will help you -

   He will uphold you with His righteous hand -

My Response

Week 3

Prayer focus for this week: Spend time praying for your friends.

	Praying	Praise
Monday		
Tuesday		
Wednesday		
Thursday		
Friday		

But we have this treasure in jars of clay, to show that the surpassing power belongs to God and not to us.

2 CORINTHIANS 4:7

Scripture for Week 3

SARAH - INFERTILITY

MONDAY

GENESIS 17:15-19

[15] And God said to Abraham, "As for Sarai your wife, you shall not call her name Sarai, but Sarah shall be her name. [16] I will bless her, and moreover, I will give you a son by her. I will bless her, and she shall become nations; kings of peoples shall come from her." [17] Then Abraham fell on his face and laughed and said to himself, "Shall a child be born to a man who is a hundred years old? Shall Sarah, who is ninety years old, bear a child?" [18] And Abraham said to God, "Oh that Ishmael might live before you!" [19] God said, "No, but Sarah your wife shall bear you a son, and you shall call his name Isaac. I will establish my covenant with him as an everlasting covenant for his offspring after him.

GENESIS 18:9-15

[9] They said to him, "Where is Sarah your wife?" And he said, "She is in the tent." [10] The Lord said, "I will surely return to you about this time next year, and Sarah your wife shall have a son." And Sarah was listening at the tent door behind him. [11] Now Abraham and Sarah were old, advanced in years. The way of women had ceased to be with Sarah. [12] So Sarah laughed to herself, saying, "After I am worn out, and my lord is old, shall I have pleasure?" [13] The Lord said to Abraham, "Why did Sarah laugh and say, 'Shall I indeed bear a child, now that I am old?' [14] Is anything too hard for the Lord? At the appointed time I will return to you, about this time next year, and Sarah shall have a son." [15] But Sarah denied it, saying, "I did not laugh," for she was afraid. He said, "No, but you did laugh."

TUESDAY

PSALM 55

¹ Give ear to my prayer, O God,

  and hide not yourself from my plea for mercy!

² Attend to me, and answer me;

  I am restless in my complaint and I moan,

³ because of the noise of the enemy,

  because of the oppression of the wicked.

For they drop trouble upon me,

  and in anger they bear a grudge against me.

⁴ My heart is in anguish within me;

  the terrors of death have fallen upon me.

⁵ Fear and trembling come upon me,

  and horror overwhelms me.

⁶ And I say, "Oh, that I had wings like a dove!

  I would fly away and be at rest;

⁷ yes, I would wander far away;

  I would lodge in the wilderness; Selah

⁸ I would hurry to find a shelter

  from the raging wind and tempest."

⁹ Destroy, O Lord, divide their tongues;

  for I see violence and strife in the city.

¹⁰ Day and night they go around it

  on its walls,

and iniquity and trouble are within it;

¹¹ ruin is in its midst;

oppression and fraud

  do not depart from its marketplace.

¹² For it is not an enemy who taunts me—

  then I could bear it;

it is not an adversary who deals insolently with me—
   then I could hide from him.
¹³ But it is you, a man, my equal,
   my companion, my familiar friend.
¹⁴ We used to take sweet counsel together;
   within God's house we walked in the throng.
¹⁵ Let death steal over them;
   let them go down to Sheol alive;
   for evil is in their dwelling place and in their heart.
¹⁶ But I call to God,
   and the Lord will save me.
¹⁷ Evening and morning and at noon
   I utter my complaint and moan,
   and he hears my voice.
¹⁸ He redeems my soul in safety
   from the battle that I wage,
   for many are arrayed against me.
¹⁹ God will give ear and humble them,
   he who is enthroned from of old, Selah
because they do not change
   and do not fear God.
²⁰ My companion stretched out his hand against his friends;
   he violated his covenant.
²¹ His speech was smooth as butter,
   yet war was in his heart;
his words were softer than oil,
   yet they were drawn swords.
²² Cast your burden on the Lord,
   and he will sustain you;
he will never permit

the righteous to be moved.

²³ But you, O God, will cast them down

  into the pit of destruction;

men of blood and treachery

  shall not live out half their days.

But I will trust in you.

WEDNESDAY

PSALM 73

¹ Truly God is good to Israel,

  to those who are pure in heart.

² But as for me, my feet had almost stumbled,

  my steps had nearly slipped.

³ For I was envious of the arrogant

  when I saw the prosperity of the wicked.

⁴ For they have no pangs until death;

  their bodies are fat and sleek.

⁵ They are not in trouble as others are;

  they are not stricken like the rest of mankind.

⁶ Therefore pride is their necklace;

  violence covers them as a garment.

⁷ Their eyes swell out through fatness;

  their hearts overflow with follies.

⁸ They scoff and speak with malice;

  loftily they threaten oppression.

⁹ They set their mouths against the heavens,

  and their tongue struts through the earth.

¹⁰ Therefore his people turn back to them,

  and find no fault in them.

¹¹ And they say, "How can God know?

Is there knowledge in the Most High?"

¹² Behold, these are the wicked;

  always at ease, they increase in riches.

¹³ All in vain have I kept my heart clean

  and washed my hands in innocence.

¹⁴ For all the day long I have been stricken

  and rebuked every morning.

¹⁵ If I had said, "I will speak thus,"

  I would have betrayed the generation of your children.

¹⁶ But when I thought how to understand this,

  it seemed to me a wearisome task,

¹⁷ until I went into the sanctuary of God;

  then I discerned their end.

¹⁸ Truly you set them in slippery places;

  you make them fall to ruin.

¹⁹ How they are destroyed in a moment,

  swept away utterly by terrors!

²⁰ Like a dream when one awakes,

  O Lord, when you rouse yourself, you despise them as phantoms.

²¹ When my soul was embittered,

  when I was pricked in heart,

²² I was brutish and ignorant;

  I was like a beast toward you.

²³ Nevertheless, I am continually with you;

  you hold my right hand.

²⁴ You guide me with your counsel,

  and afterward you will receive me to glory.

²⁵ Whom have I in heaven but you?

  And there is nothing on earth that I desire besides you.

²⁶ My flesh and my heart may fail,

but God is the strength of my heart and my portion forever.

²⁷ For behold, those who are far from you shall perish;

you put an end to everyone who is unfaithful to you.

²⁸ But for me it is good to be near God;

I have made the Lord God my refuge,

that I may tell of all your works.

THURSDAY

PSALM 119:68

⁶⁸ You are good and do good;

teach me your statutes.

PSALM 34:8-11

⁸ Oh, taste and see that the Lord is good!

Blessed is the man who takes refuge in him!

⁹ Oh, fear the Lord, you his saints,

for those who fear him have no lack!

¹⁰ The young lions suffer want and hunger;

but those who seek the Lord lack no good thing.

¹¹ Come, O children, listen to me;

I will teach you the fear of the Lord.

FRIDAY

2 CORINTHIANS 4:7-11

⁷ But we have this treasure in jars of clay, to show that the surpassing power belongs to God and not to us. ⁸ We are afflicted in every way, but not crushed; perplexed, but not driven to despair; ⁹ persecuted, but not forsaken; struck down, but not destroyed; ¹⁰ always carrying in the body the death of Jesus, so that the life of Jesus may also be manifested in our bodies. ¹¹ For we who live are always being given over to death for Jesus' sake, so that the life of Jesus also may be manifested in our mortal flesh.

Monday

READ: Genesis 17:15-19; Genesis 18:9-15

SOAP: Genesis 18:12-14a

Scripture - Write out the **Scripture** passage for the day.

Observations - Write down 1 or 2 **observations** from the passage.

Monday

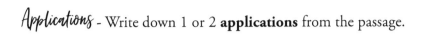

Applications - Write down 1 or 2 **applications** from the passage.

Pray - Write out a **prayer** over what you learned from today's passage.

-Visit our website today for the corresponding blog post!-

Tuesday

READ: Psalm 55

SOAP: Psalm 55:22

Scripture - Write out the **Scripture** passage for the day.

Observations - Write down 1 or 2 **observations** from the passage.

Tuesday

Applications - Write down 1 or 2 **applications** from the passage.

Pray - Write out a **prayer** over what you learned from today's passage.

Wednesday

READ: Psalm 73
SOAP: Psalm 73:25-26

Scripture - Write out the **Scripture** passage for the day.

Observations - Write down 1 or 2 **observations** from the passage.

Wednesday

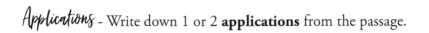

Applications - Write down 1 or 2 **applications** from the passage.

Pray - Write out a **prayer** over what you learned from today's passage.

-Visit our website today for the corresponding blog post!-

Thursday

READ: Psalm 119:68; Psalm 34:8-11
SOAP: Psalm 119:68

Scripture - Write out the **Scripture** passage for the day.

Observations - Write down 1 or 2 **observations** from the passage.

Thursday

Applications - Write down 1 or 2 **applications** from the passage.

Pray - Write out a **prayer** over what you learned from today's passage.

Friday

READ: 2 Corinthians 4:7-11
SOAP: 2 Corinthians 4:7-9

Scripture - Write out the **Scripture** passage for the day.

Observations - Write down 1 or 2 **observations** from the passage.

Friday

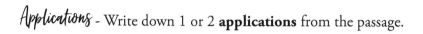

Applications - Write down 1 or 2 **applications** from the passage.

Pray - Write out a **prayer** over what you learned from today's passage.

-Visit our website today for the corresponding blog post!-

Reflection Questions

1. Why did Sarah laugh?

2. What burdens do you have a hard time "casting on the Lord"?

3. What does it mean for God to be sufficient?

4. What does it mean that God is good, and how does this apply to those struggling with infertility?

5. This world is very broken. We are broken. How is it that we are able to bear this brokenness without being crushed, perplexed, or driven to despair?

My Response

Week 4

Week 4 Challenge (Note: You can find this listed in our Monday blog post):

Prayer focus for this week: Spend time praying for your church.

	Praying	Praise
Monday		
Tuesday		
Wednesday		
Thursday		
Friday		

so that, as it is written,
"Let the one who boasts,
boast in the Lord."

1 CORINTHIANS 1:31

Scripture for Week 4

PAUL - MISPLACED ZEAL AND PRIDE

MONDAY

GALATIANS 1:11-14

¹¹ For I would have you know, brothers, that the gospel that was preached by me is not man's gospel. ¹² For I did not receive it from any man, nor was I taught it, but I received it through a revelation of Jesus Christ. ¹³ For you have heard of my former life in Judaism, how I persecuted the church of God violently and tried to destroy it.¹⁴ And I was advancing in Judaism beyond many of my own age among my people, so extremely zealous was I for the traditions of my fathers.

TUESDAY

GALATIANS 6:11-16

¹¹ See with what large letters I am writing to you with my own hand.¹² It is those who want to make a good showing in the flesh who would force you to be circumcised, and only in order that they may not be persecuted for the cross of Christ. ¹³ For even those who are circumcised do not themselves keep the law, but they desire to have you circumcised that they may boast in your flesh. ¹⁴ But far be it from me to boast except in the cross of our Lord Jesus Christ, by which the world has been crucified to me, and I to the world. ¹⁵ For neither circumcision counts for anything, nor uncircumcision, but a new creation. ¹⁶ And as for all who walk by this rule, peace and mercy be upon them, and upon the Israel of God.

WEDNESDAY

1 CORINTHIANS 1:26-31

²⁶ For consider your calling, brothers: not many of you were wise according to worldly standards, not many were powerful, not many were of noble birth. ²⁷ But God chose what is foolish in the

world to shame the wise; God chose what is weak in the world to shame the strong; [28] God chose what is low and despised in the world, even things that are not, to bring to nothing things that are, [29] so that no human being might boast in the presence of God. [30] And because of him you are in Christ Jesus, who became to us wisdom from God, righteousness and sanctification and redemption, [31] so that, as it is written, "Let the one who boasts, boast in the Lord."

THURSDAY

JAMES 4:6-10

[6] But he gives more grace. Therefore it says, "God opposes the proud but gives grace to the humble." [7] Submit yourselves therefore to God. Resist the devil, and he will flee from you. [8] Draw near to God, and he will draw near to you. Cleanse your hands, you sinners, and purify your hearts, you double-minded. [9] Be wretched and mourn and weep. Let your laughter be turned to mourning and your joy to gloom. [10] Humble yourselves before the Lord, and he will exalt you.

FRIDAY

TITUS 2:11-14

[11] For the grace of God has appeared, bringing salvation for all people, [12] training us to renounce ungodliness and worldly passions, and to live self-controlled, upright, and godly lives in the present age, [13] waiting for our blessed hope, the appearing of the glory of our great God and Savior Jesus Christ, [14] who gave himself for us to redeem us from all lawlessness and to purify for himself a people for his own possession who are zealous for good works.

Monday

READ: Galatians 1:11-14
SOAP: Galatians 1:14

Scripture - Write out the **Scripture** passage for the day.

Observations - Write down 1 or 2 **observations** from the passage.

Monday

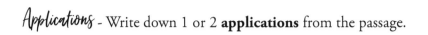

Applications - Write down 1 or 2 **applications** from the passage.

Pray - Write out a **prayer** over what you learned from today's passage.

-Visit our website today for the corresponding blog post!-

Tuesday

READ: Galatians 6:11-16
SOAP: Galatians 6:14-15

Scripture - Write out the **Scripture** passage for the day.

Observations - Write down 1 or 2 **observations** from the passage.

Tuesday

Applications - Write down 1 or 2 **applications** from the passage.

Pray - Write out a **prayer** over what you learned from today's passage.

Wednesday

READ: 1 Corinthians 1:26-31

SOAP: 1 Corinthians 1:30-31

Scripture - Write out the **Scripture** passage for the day.

Observations - Write down 1 or 2 **observations** from the passage.

Wednesday

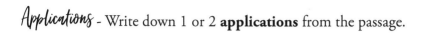

Applications - Write down 1 or 2 **applications** from the passage.

Pray - Write out a **prayer** over what you learned from today's passage.

-Visit our website today for the corresponding blog post!-

Thursday

READ: James 4:6-10
SOAP: James 4:6

Scripture - Write out the **Scripture** passage for the day.

Observations - Write down 1 or 2 **observations** from the passage.

Thursday

Applications - Write down 1 or 2 **applications** from the passage.

Pray - Write out a **prayer** over what you learned from today's passage.

Friday

READ: Titus 2:11-14
SOAP: Titus 2:14

Scripture - Write out the **Scripture** passage for the day.

Observations - Write down 1 or 2 **observations** from the passage.

Friday

Applications - Write down 1 or 2 **applications** from the passage.

Pray - Write out a **prayer** over what you learned from today's passage.

-Visit our website today for the corresponding blog post!-

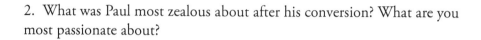

Reflection Questions

1. What does zeal mean? Before his conversion, what was Paul most zealous about?

2. What was Paul most zealous about after his conversion? What are you most passionate about?

3. What does it mean to boast? What are we to boast about? How do we do that?

4. How does God oppose the proud? How does He give grace to those who are humble?

5. What good works are we to be zealous for?

My Response

Week 5

Week 5 Challenge (Note: You can find this listed in our Monday blog post):

Prayer focus for this week: Spend time praying for missionaries.

	Praying	Praise
Monday		
Tuesday		
Wednesday		
Thursday		
Friday		

There is therefore now no condemnation for those who are in Christ Jesus. For the law of the Spirit of life has set you free in Christ Jesus from the law of sin and death.

ROMANS 8:1-2

Scripture for Week 5

THE ADULTEROUS WOMAN

MONDAY

JOHN 8:1-11

[1] but Jesus went to the Mount of Olives. [2] Early in the morning he came again to the temple. All the people came to him, and he sat down and taught them. [3] The scribes and the Pharisees brought a woman who had been caught in adultery, and placing her in the midst [4] they said to him, "Teacher, this woman has been caught in the act of adultery. [5] Now in the Law, Moses commanded us to stone such women. So what do you say?" [6] This they said to test him, that they might have some charge to bring against him. Jesus bent down and wrote with his finger on the ground. [7] And as they continued to ask him, he stood up and said to them, "Let him who is without sin among you be the first to throw a stone at her." [8] And once more he bent down and wrote on the ground. [9] But when they heard it, they went away one by one, beginning with the older ones, and Jesus was left alone with the woman standing before him. [10] Jesus stood up and said to her, "Woman, where are they? Has no one condemned you?" [11] She said, "No one, Lord." And Jesus said, "Neither do I condemn you; go, and from now on sin no more."

TUESDAY

ROMANS 8:1-11

[1] There is therefore now no condemnation for those who are in Christ Jesus. [2] For the law of the Spirit of life has set you free in Christ Jesus from the law of sin and death. [3] For God has done what the law, weakened by the flesh, could not do. By sending his own Son in the likeness of sinful flesh and for sin, he condemned sin in the flesh, [4] in order that the righteous requirement of the law might be fulfilled in us, who walk not according to the flesh but according to the Spirit. [5] For those who live according to the flesh set their minds on the things of the flesh, but those who

live according to the Spirit set their minds on the things of the Spirit. ⁶ For to set the mind on the flesh is death, but to set the mind on the Spirit is life and peace. ⁷ For the mind that is set on the flesh is hostile to God, for it does not submit to God's law; indeed, it cannot. ⁸ Those who are in the flesh cannot please God.

⁹ You, however, are not in the flesh but in the Spirit, if in fact the Spirit of God dwells in you. Anyone who does not have the Spirit of Christ does not belong to him. ¹⁰ But if Christ is in you, although the body is dead because of sin, the Spirit is life because of righteousness. ¹¹ If the Spirit of him who raised Jesus from the dead dwells in you, he who raised Christ Jesus from the dead will also give life to your mortal bodies through his Spirit who dwells in you.

WEDNESDAY

PSALM 103

¹ Bless the Lord, O my soul,

and all that is within me,

bless his holy name!

² Bless the Lord, O my soul,

and forget not all his benefits,

³ who forgives all your iniquity,

who heals all your diseases,

⁴ who redeems your life from the pit,

who crowns you with steadfast love and mercy,

⁵ who satisfies you with good

so that your youth is renewed like the eagle's.

⁶ The Lord works righteousness

and justice for all who are oppressed.

⁷ He made known his ways to Moses,

his acts to the people of Israel.

[8] The Lord is merciful and gracious,

   slow to anger and abounding in steadfast love.

[9] He will not always chide,

   nor will he keep his anger forever.

[10] He does not deal with us according to our sins,

   nor repay us according to our iniquities.

[11] For as high as the heavens are above the earth,

   so great is his steadfast love toward those who fear him;

[12] as far as the east is from the west,

   so far does he remove our transgressions from us.

[13] As a father shows compassion to his children,

   so the Lord shows compassion to those who fear him.

[14] For he knows our frame;

   he remembers that we are dust.

[15] As for man, his days are like grass;

   he flourishes like a flower of the field;

[16] for the wind passes over it, and it is gone,

   and its place knows it no more.

[17] But the steadfast love of the Lord is from everlasting to everlasting
on those who fear him,

   and his righteousness to children's children,

[18] to those who keep his covenant

   and remember to do his commandments.

[19] The Lord has established his throne in the heavens,

   and his kingdom rules over all.

[20] Bless the Lord, O you his angels,

   you mighty ones who do his word,

   obeying the voice of his word!

[21] Bless the Lord, all his hosts,

his ministers, who do his will!

²² Bless the Lord, all his works,

in all places of his dominion.

Bless the Lord, O my soul!

THURSDAY

PSALM 27

¹ The Lord is my light and my salvation;

whom shall I fear?

The Lord is the stronghold of my life;

of whom shall I be afraid?

² When evildoers assail me

to eat up my flesh,

my adversaries and foes,

it is they who stumble and fall.

³ Though an army encamp against me,

my heart shall not fear;

though war arise against me,

yet I will be confident.

⁴ One thing have I asked of the Lord,

that will I seek after:

that I may dwell in the house of the Lord

all the days of my life,

to gaze upon the beauty of the Lord

and to inquire in his temple.

⁵ For he will hide me in his shelter

in the day of trouble;

he will conceal me under the cover of his tent;

he will lift me high upon a rock.

⁶ And now my head shall be lifted up

above my enemies all around me,
and I will offer in his tent
   sacrifices with shouts of joy;
I will sing and make melody to the Lord.
[7] Hear, O Lord, when I cry aloud;
   be gracious to me and answer me!
[8] You have said, "Seek my face."
My heart says to you,
   "Your face, Lord, do I seek."
[9]   Hide not your face from me.
Turn not your servant away in anger,
   O you who have been my help.
Cast me not off; forsake me not,
   O God of my salvation!
[10] For my father and my mother have forsaken me,
   but the Lord will take me in.
[11] Teach me your way, O Lord,
   and lead me on a level path
   because of my enemies.
[12] Give me not up to the will of my adversaries;
   for false witnesses have risen against me,
   and they breathe out violence.
[13] I believe that I shall look upon the goodness of the Lord
   in the land of the living!
[14] Wait for the Lord;
   be strong, and let your heart take courage;
   wait for the Lord!

FRIDAY

JAMES 4:1-4

[1] What causes quarrels and what causes fights among you? Is it not this, that your passions are at war within you? [2] You desire and do not have, so you murder. You covet and cannot obtain, so you fight and quarrel. You do not have, because you do not ask. [3] You ask and do not receive, because you ask wrongly, to spend it on your passions. [4] You adulterous people! Do you not know that friendship with the world is enmity with God? Therefore whoever wishes to be a friend of the world makes himself an enemy of God.

Monday

READ: John 8:1-11
SOAP: John 8:10-11

Scripture - Write out the **Scripture** passage for the day.

Observations - Write down 1 or 2 **observations** from the passage.

Monday

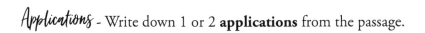

Applications - Write down 1 or 2 **applications** from the passage.

Pray - Write out a **prayer** over what you learned from today's passage.

-Visit our website today for the corresponding blog post!-

Tuesday

READ: Romans 8:1-11
SOAP: Romans 8:1-2

Scripture - Write out the **Scripture** passage for the day.

Observations - Write down 1 or 2 **observations** from the passage.

Tuesday

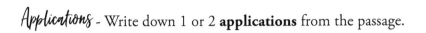

Applications - Write down 1 or 2 **applications** from the passage.

Pray - Write out a **prayer** over what you learned from today's passage.

Wednesday

READ: Psalm 103

SOAP: Psalm 103:11-13

Scripture - Write out the **Scripture** passage for the day.

Observations - Write down 1 or 2 **observations** from the passage.

Wednesday

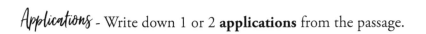

Applications - Write down 1 or 2 **applications** from the passage.

Pray - Write out a **prayer** over what you learned from today's passage.

-Visit our website today for the corresponding blog post!-

Thursday

READ: Psalm 27
SOAP: Psalm 27:7-8

Scripture - Write out the **Scripture** passage for the day.

Observations - Write down 1 or 2 **observations** from the passage.

Thursday

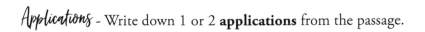

Applications - Write down 1 or 2 **applications** from the passage.

Pray - Write out a **prayer** over what you learned from today's passage.

Friday

READ: James 4:1-4

SOAP: James 4:4

Scripture - Write out the **Scripture** passage for the day.

Observations - Write down 1 or 2 **observations** from the passage.

Friday

Applications - Write down 1 or 2 **applications** from the passage.

Pray - Write out a **prayer** over what you learned from today's passage.

-Visit our website today for the corresponding blog post!-

Reflection Questions

1. Why did Jesus not condemn the adulterous woman? What did He tell her to do?

2. "There is therefore now no condemnation for those who are in Christ Jesus." What does this mean regarding our past?

3. How deep is our sin problem? How much has God forgiven us?

4. While God, through Jesus, has offered us complete forgiveness, He also instructs us in the way we are to live. How do we learn His ways?

5. How do we commit adultery with the world? What does it mean to stay faithful to God?

My Response

Week 6

Week 6 Challenge (Note: You can find this listed in our Monday blog post):

Prayer focus for this week: Spend time praying for you.

	Praying	Praise
Monday		
Tuesday		
Wednesday		
Thursday		
Friday		

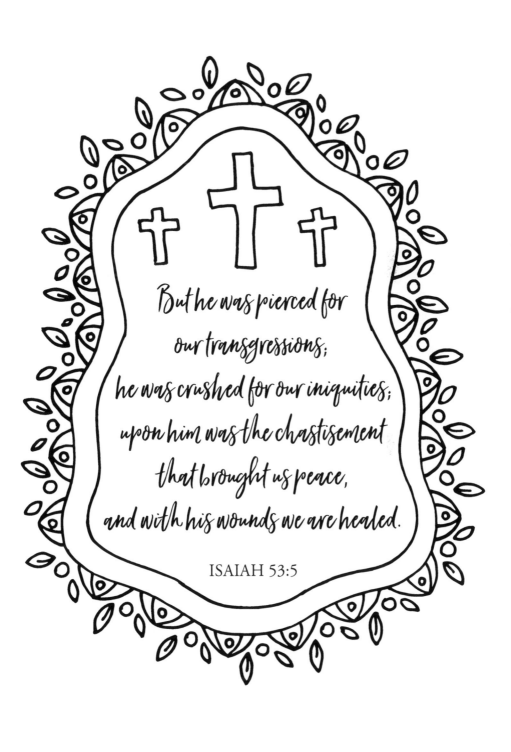

But he was pierced for our transgressions; he was crushed for our iniquities; upon him was the chastisement that brought us peace, and with his wounds we are healed.

ISAIAH 53:5

JESUS - BROKEN AND RAISED FOR US

MONDAY

ISAIAH 53

1 Who has believed what he has heard from us?
  And to whom has the arm of the Lord been revealed?
2 For he grew up before him like a young plant,
  and like a root out of dry ground;
he had no form or majesty that we should look at him,
  and no beauty that we should desire him.
3 He was despised and rejected by men,
  a man of sorrows and acquainted with grief;
and as one from whom men hide their faces
  he was despised, and we esteemed him not.
4 Surely he has borne our griefs
  and carried our sorrows;
yet we esteemed him stricken,
  smitten by God, and afflicted.
5 But he was pierced for our transgressions;
  he was crushed for our iniquities;
upon him was the chastisement that brought us peace,
  and with his wounds we are healed.
6 All we like sheep have gone astray;
  we have turned—every one—to his own way;
and the Lord has laid on him
  the iniquity of us all.
7 He was oppressed, and he was afflicted,

yet he opened not his mouth;
like a lamb that is led to the slaughter,
    and like a sheep that before its shearers is silent,
    so he opened not his mouth.
8 By oppression and judgment he was taken away;
    and as for his generation, who considered
that he was cut off out of the land of the living,
    stricken for the transgression of my people?
9 And they made his grave with the wicked
    and with a rich man in his death,
although he had done no violence,
    and there was no deceit in his mouth.
10 Yet it was the will of the Lord to crush him;
    he has put him to grief;
when his soul makes an offering for guilt,
    he shall see his offspring; he shall prolong his days;
the will of the Lord shall prosper in his hand.
11 Out of the anguish of his soul he shall see and be satisfied;
by his knowledge shall the righteous one, my servant,
    make many to be accounted righteous,
    and he shall bear their iniquities.
12 Therefore I will divide him a portion with the many,
    and he shall divide the spoil with the strong,
because he poured out his soul to death
    and was numbered with the transgressors;
yet he bore the sin of many,
    and makes intercession for the transgressors.

TUESDAY

MATTHEW 26:17-29

[17] Now on the first day of Unleavened Bread the disciples came to Jesus, saying, "Where will you have us prepare for you to eat the Passover?" [18] He said, "Go into the city to a certain man and say to him, 'The Teacher says, My time is at hand. I will keep the Passover at your house with my disciples.'" [19] And the disciples did as Jesus had directed them, and they prepared the Passover.

[20] When it was evening, he reclined at table with the twelve. [21] And as they were eating, he said, "Truly, I say to you, one of you will betray me." [22] And they were very sorrowful and began to say to him one after another, "Is it I, Lord?" [23] He answered, "He who has dipped his hand in the dish with me will betray me. [24] The Son of Man goes as it is written of him, but woe to that man by whom the Son of Man is betrayed! It would have been better for that man if he had not been born." [25] Judas, who would betray him, answered, "Is it I, Rabbi?" He said to him, "You have said so."

[26] Now as they were eating, Jesus took bread, and after blessing it broke it and gave it to the disciples, and said, "Take, eat; this is my body." [27] And he took a cup, and when he had given thanks he gave it to them, saying, "Drink of it, all of you, [28] for this is my blood of the covenant, which is poured out for many for the forgiveness of sins. [29] I tell you I will not drink again of this fruit of the vine until that day when I drink it new with you in my Father's kingdom."

WEDNESDAY

JOHN 19:16-30

[16] So he delivered him over to them to be crucified.

So they took Jesus, [17] and he went out, bearing his own cross, to the place called The Place of a Skull, which in Aramaic is called Golgotha. [18] There they crucified him, and with him two others, one on either side, and Jesus between them. [19] Pilate also wrote an inscription and put it on the cross. It read, "Jesus of Nazareth, the King of the Jews." [20] Many of the Jews read this inscription, for the place where Jesus was crucified was near the city, and it was written in Aramaic, in Latin, and in Greek. ²¹ So the chief priests of the Jews said to Pilate, "Do not write, 'The King of the Jews,' but rather, 'This man said, I am King of the Jews.'" ²² Pilate answered, "What I have written I have written."

²³ When the soldiers had crucified Jesus, they took his garments and divided them into four parts, one part for each soldier; also his tunic. But the tunic was seamless, woven in one piece from top to bottom, ²⁴ so they said to one another, "Let us not tear it, but cast lots for it to see whose it shall be." This was to fulfill the Scripture which says,

"They divided my garments among them,

and for my clothing they cast lots."

So the soldiers did these things, ²⁵ but standing by the cross of Jesus were his mother and his mother's sister, Mary the wife of Clopas, and Mary Magdalene. ²⁶ When Jesus saw his mother and the disciple whom he loved standing nearby, he said to his mother, "Woman, behold, your son!" ²⁷ Then he said to the disciple, "Behold, your mother!" And from that hour the disciple took her to his own home.

²⁸ After this, Jesus, knowing that all was now finished, said (to fulfill the Scripture), "I thirst." ²⁹ A jar full of sour wine stood there, so they put a sponge full of the sour wine on a hyssop branch and held it to his mouth. ³⁰ When Jesus had received the sour wine, he said, "It is finished," and he bowed his head and gave up his spirit.

THURSDAY

HEBREWS 12:1-3

¹ Therefore, since we are surrounded by so great a cloud of witnesses, let us also lay aside every weight, and sin which clings so closely, and let us run with endurance the race that is set before us,² looking to Jesus, the founder and perfecter of our faith, who for the joy that was set before him endured the cross, despising the shame, and is seated at the right hand of the throne of God.

³ Consider him who endured from sinners such hostility against himself, so that you may not grow weary or fainthearted.

FRIDAY

1 CORINTHIANS 15:1-4

¹ Now I would remind you, brothers, of the gospel I preached to you, which you received, in which you stand, ² and by which you are being saved, if you hold fast to the word I preached to you—unless you believed in vain.

³ For I delivered to you as of first importance what I also received: that Christ died for our sins in accordance with the Scriptures, ⁴ that he was buried, that he was raised on the third day in accordance with the Scriptures,

Monday

READ: Isaiah 53
SOAP: Isaiah 53:4-5

Scripture - Write out the **Scripture** passage for the day.

Observations - Write down 1 or 2 **observations** from the passage.

Monday

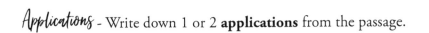

Applications - Write down 1 or 2 **applications** from the passage.

Pray - Write out a **prayer** over what you learned from today's passage.

-Visit our website today for the corresponding blog post!-

Tuesday

READ: Matthew 26:17-29

SOAP: Matthew 26:26-27

Scripture - Write out the **Scripture** passage for the day.

Observations - Write down 1 or 2 **observations** from the passage.

Tuesday

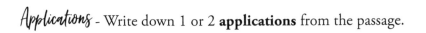

Applications - Write down 1 or 2 **applications** from the passage.

Pray - Write out a **prayer** over what you learned from today's passage.

Wednesday

READ: John 19:16-30
SOAP: John 19:28-30

Scripture - Write out the **Scripture** passage for the day.

Observations - Write down 1 or 2 **observations** from the passage.

Wednesday

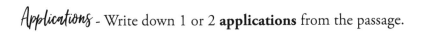

Applications - Write down 1 or 2 **applications** from the passage.

Pray - Write out a **prayer** over what you learned from today's passage.

-Visit our website today for the corresponding blog post!-

Thursday

READ: Hebrews 12:1-3
SOAP: Hebrews 12:3

Scripture - Write out the **Scripture** passage for the day.

Observations - Write down 1 or 2 **observations** from the passage.

Thursday

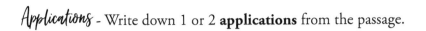

Applications - Write down 1 or 2 **applications** from the passage.

Pray - Write out a **prayer** over what you learned from today's passage.

Friday

READ: 1 Corinthians 15:1-4
SOAP: 1 Corinthians 15:3-4

Scripture - Write out the **Scripture** passage for the day.

Observations - Write down 1 or 2 **observations** from the passage.

Friday

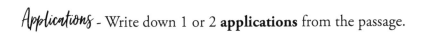

Applications - Write down 1 or 2 **applications** from the passage.

Pray - Write out a **prayer** over what you learned from today's passage.

-Visit our website today for the corresponding blog post!-

Reflection Questions

1. In what ways was Jesus broken for us?

2. Why did Jesus implement the ordinance of communion?

3. When Jesus said, "It is finished," what did He mean?

4. How do Jesus' sufferings and death keep us from getting "weary and fainthearted"?

5. Why is the death and resurrection of Jesus of "first importance"? What does this mean for our priorities?

My Response

Know these truths from God's Word...

God loves you.

Even when you're feeling unworthy and like the world is stacked against you, God loves you - *yes, you* - and He has created you for great purpose.

> God's Word says, "God so loved the world that He gave His one and only Son, Jesus, that whoever believes in Him shall not perish, but have eternal life" (John 3:16).

Our sin separates us from God.

We are all sinners by nature and by choice, and because of this we are separated from God, who is holy.

> God's Word says, "All have sinned and fall short of the glory of God" (Romans 3:23).

Jesus died so that you might have life.

The consequence of sin is death, but your story doesn't have to end there! God's free gift of salvation is available to us because Jesus took the penalty for our sin when He died on the cross.

> God's Word says, "For the wages of sin is death, but the free gift of

God is eternal life in Christ Jesus our Lord" (Romans 6:23); "God demonstrates His own love toward us, in that while we were yet sinners, Christ died for us" (Romans 5:8).

Jesus lives!

Death could not hold Him, and three days after His body was placed in the tomb Jesus rose again, defeating sin and death forever! He lives today in heaven and is preparing a place in eternity for all who believe in Him.

God's Word says, "In my Father's house are many rooms. If it were not so, would I have told you that I go to prepare a place for you? And if I go and prepare a place for you, I will come again and will take you to myself, that where I am you may be also" (John 14:2-3).

Yes, you can KNOW that you are forgiven.

Accept Jesus as the only way to salvation…

Accepting Jesus as your Savior is not about what you can do, but rather about having faith in what Jesus has already done. It takes recognizing that you are a sinner, believing that Jesus died for your sins, and asking for forgiveness by placing your full trust in Jesus's work on the cross on your behalf.

God's Word says, "If you confess with your mouth that Jesus is Lord and believe in your heart that God raised him from the dead, you will be saved. For with the heart one believes and is justified, and with the mouth one confesses and is saved" (Romans 10:9-10).

Practically, what does that look like? With a sincere heart, you can pray a simple prayer like this:

God,

I know that I am a sinner.

I don't want to live another day without embracing

the love and forgiveness that You have for me.

I ask for Your forgiveness.

I believe that You died for my sins and rose from the dead.

I surrender all that I am and ask You to be Lord of my life.

Help me to turn from my sin and follow You.

Teach me what it means to walk in freedom as I live under Your grace,

and help me to grow in Your ways as I seek to know You more.

Amen.

If you just prayed this prayer (or something similar in your own words), would you email us at info@lovegodgreatly.com? We'd love to help get you started on this exciting journey as a child of God!

Welcome, friend. We're so glad you're here...

LOVE GOD GREATLY exists to inspire, encourage, and equip women all over the world to make God's Word a priority in their lives.

-INSPIRE-

women to make God's Word a priority in their daily lives through our Bible study resources.

-ENCOURAGE-

women in their daily walks with God through online community and personal accountability.

-EQUIP-

women to grow in their faith, so that they can effectively reach others for Christ.

Love God Greatly consists of a beautiful community of women who use a variety of technology platforms to keep each other accountable in God's Word.

We start with a simple Bible reading plan, but it doesn't stop there.

Some gather in homes and churches locally, while others connect online with women across the globe. Whatever the method, we lovingly lock arms and unite for this purpose...

to Love God Greatly with our lives.

At *Love God Greatly*, you'll find real, authentic women. Women who are imperfect, yet forgiven. Women who desire less of us, and a whole lot more of Jesus. Women who long to know God through his Word, because we know that Truth transforms and sets us free. **Women who are better together, saturated in God's Word and in community with one another.**

Love God Greatly is a 501 (C) (3) non-profit organization. Funding for Love God Greatly comes through donations and proceeds from our online Bible study journals and books. LGG is committed to providing quality Bible study materials and believes finances should never get in the way of a woman being able to participate in one of our studies. All LGG journals and translated journals are available to download for free from LoveGodGreatly.com for those who cannot afford to purchase them. Our journals and books are also available for sale on Amazon. Search for "Love God Greatly" to see all of our Bible study journals and books. 100% of proceeds go directly back into supporting Love God Greatly and helping us inspire, encourage and equip women all over the world with God's Word.

THANK YOU for partnering with us!

What we offer:

18 + Translations | Bible Reading Plans | Online Bible Study
Love God Greatly App | 80 + Countries Served
Bible Study Journals & Books | Community Groups

Each Love God Greatly study includes:

Three Devotional Corresponding Blog Posts | Monday Vlog Videos
Memory Verses | Weekly Challenge | Weekly Reading Plan
Reflection Questions And More!

Other Love God Greatly studies include:

David | Ecclesiastes | Growing Through Prayer | Names Of God
Galatians | Psalm 119 | 1st & 2nd Peter | Made For Community | Esther
The Road To Christmas | The Source Of Gratitude | You Are Loved

Made in the USA
Middletown, DE
05 February 2018